TRIUMPH HOUSE
Poetry with a Purpose

CHANGING SEASONS

Edited by

CHRIS WALTON

First published in Great Britain in 1999 by
TRIUMPH HOUSE
1-2 Wainman Road, Woodston,
Peterborough, PE2 7BU
Telephone (01733) 230749

All Rights Reserved

Copyright Contributors 1999

HB ISBN 1 86161 424 1
SB ISBN 1 86161 429 2

Foreword

With the continuous routine cycle from year to year, how many people actually stop to consider the wonderful changes of nature and how it affects our day-to-day lives? Each of the four seasons brings with it many of its own special characteristics (often with a few surprises) but which do you prefer? Do you love to lie basking, soaking up the sun on the long hot days of summer, or enjoy more of a night in, tucked up snugly by the fire on a cold winter's night?

The authors within this book have taken time out to share their own special feelings and preferences to the four seasons of each year, as they take you on a poetic tour of a lifetime. From the freezing fun of winter snow to the delight of new birth in spring, there is sure to be something here for everyone.

Chris Walton
Editor

Contents

Spring I Do Love	S Wall	1
Autumn Colours	Cathy Mearman	2
Transformation	Elaine Waite	3
Weeds Or Flowers	Helen Young	4
The Changing Of The Seasons	David Ford	5
Autumn	Muriel E Read	6
Change	S E Spooner	7
October Trees	Lynn Brookes	8
Autumn Lesson	Scarlett	9
Oh Earth! Oh Earth!	Ebenezer Essuman	10
A Spring Tonic	Maisie Roberts	11
God's Seasons	Fred Schofield	12
Winter-Logged	Dick Anstis	13
Spring	Doreen Hadfield	14
Summer Sails	Fredrick Caxton Holt	15
Have You Overlooked Anything Today?	Pablo Hamill Magee	16
The Snowdrop	Edward Farren	17
Springtime	S Askew	18
The Sky	Bonnie M Frier	19
1998, Mum's Summer Blues	M M Watson	20
Winter	Jill Silverman	21
The Wonders Of The Maker	Madeline Green	22
Last Summer	Sandra Davies	23
Cycle Of The Seasons	Bee Wickens	24
Cloaks Of Green	M Lloyd	25
February Pinions	J Allison	26
The Horse Chestnut Tree	Mick Moyce	27
It's Not The Same Without The Raspberry Ripple	Skye Taylor	28
Changing Seasons	Lynda Margaret Firth	29
The Fall	Marian Curtis Jones	30
Autumn Love	Tahira	31
Rocky Mountain Memories	P R McDonald	32
Autumn	Pam Owers	33

Summertime Special	T G Porter	34
Avenue, Autumn	S H Smith	35
Changing Seasons Of The Heart	Elizabeth Mark	36
Silver Threads	Betty Foot	37
Changing Seasons	Babe Morgan	38
Summer On The Foyle	Debbie Caulfield	39
Distorted Images On A Windswept Afternoon	Jim Nicholas	40
The Sea And The Seasons	Eileen Cuddy Buckley	41
Hello Winter!	Ann Beard	42
Time's Friend	J C Walters	43
Winters Long Ago	Amy Cornes Torr	44
A Walk In The Wood	Rozetta Pate	45
Snowdrops	Jill Barker	46
Winter - The Last Crop	Mark Himlin	47
Autumn	Callum Tweed	48
Spring Colours	Susan Turner	49
The Snowdrop	R T Owen	50
All This	Hazel Cullis	51
Mother Earth	Maureen Nash	52
Summer's Sadness	Jane Mills	53
Nature's Treasures	Josephine Western	54
God's Gift Of Love	Rev Harry Rolfe	55
Changing Seasons	Jean P McGovern	56
Springtime	Kathleen Spilsbury	57
The Quiet Man	Alison Forbes	58
True Love	Alma Montgomery Frank	59
Wonderful Thing Is Spring	C J Walls	60
Life's Seasons	P Rock	61
A Day To Remember	C Webb	62
Begone The Winter	Brenda Robson-Eifler	63
Changing Seasons	Catherine J MacKenzie	64
Summer	William Stannard	65
Autumn	Gabrielle Hopkins	66
Autumn	Sam Lyons	67
Winter's Song	Nancy Knight	68
Falling Leaves	P Kendrick	69
Humane Life Cycle	Ghazanfer Eqbal	70

Old Man Winter	Nan Ogg	71
Autumn's Song	Jean Parry	72
Sunday Panic	Maureen Atkin	73
Two Seasons In One	Merilyn Elizabeth Anne Gulley	74
September	Ivy E Russell	75
Feeding Time	Eva Morris	76
My Glorious Day	Ivy Blades	77
First Snow	Dennis Marshall	78
Changing Seasons	Sue Knight	79
A Walk On The Wild Side	Lynda Burton	80
The Best Excuse	Barbara Sherlow	81
The Coals	Jackie Hyde	82
Seasons' Treasured Moments	Mai Clarke	83
Summer Is Here	Dorothy Whitehall	84
Autumn	Joyce Mussett	85
Autumn Pleasures	Marjorie Cowan	86
A Garden Thought	Nancy Owen	87
Haiku Seasons	Marion Evans	88
Winter's Hope	Barrie W Neate	90
Beautiful Autumn	Pat Heppel	91
Nature's Wonders	Valerie Baker	92
The Four Seasons	Roger Williams	93
Snow In Winter	Lynne Heather West	94
Wings And Things	Pam Dawkins	95
Autumn Dawn	David J Burke	96
Season's Reasons	G Gray	97
They Tell Me Spring Is Beautiful	Eileen N Blackmore	98
Autumn	Ruth Dewhirst	99
Changing Season	E Snell	100
The Fall	B King	101
Autumn	Andrew Whitfield	102
Autumn Leaves	John Hickman	103

SPRING I DO LOVE

To see those snowdrops peeping thro'
To see those branches, sprouting leaves
To feel the air so light and still
To know that winter has left us once again
The chill in the air lingers still
But the flowers will soon flourish
And the skies will be blue
The birds start to tweet
New ones are born
Then the robin hops down
And pays a call
That is the reason I like the spring
To watch things grow
Is a wonderful thing.

S Wall

AUTUMN COLOURS

Red, orange, yellow, brown
- these are the colours of autumn.
The hazy days of summer now gone,
school holidays are over,
evenings are drawing in.

Clocks go back one hour,
bonfires are lit and we brighten the sky
with colourful displays of fireworks.
Shopping days to Christmas are numbered
and we make lists of cards and presents to buy.

I like autumn because of the colours.
Every tree has its own pattern of leaves
which fall one by one to form a carpet on the ground.

It reminds me of the preciousness of life;
Each tiny new-born baby is a special gift
from our Creator God who made every living thing,
sustaining it with His protecting hand,
guiding and helping it to fulfil its own potential.

Cathy Mearman

TRANSFORMATION

T he winter winds have abated.
R ising sun now bathes the land with warmth.
A nimals wake from their long winter sleep.
N urturing the young which have been born.
S nows have long past,
F rozen lands thaw.
O vercast days break to reveal blue spring skies.
R ivers sparkle with fresh water.
M arshlands alive with migrating birds.
A ll flora bursts into life,
T o reveal a carpet of colour and smell.
I n a matter of months we will have forgotten,
O vercast days, snow and biting winds,
N ow spring has arrived.

Elaine Waite

WEEDS OR FLOWERS

New cut grass fresh and green
Not a weed there can be seen
But just a shower of summer rain
The daisies soon show up again
They quickly spread across the lawn
As they open their eyes to the morning sun
Weeds said the man
Flowers said the child
God's own garden growing wild
A buttercup too gold like the sun
Joins the daisies on the lawn
And a dandelion bright and yellow
Raised his head that dandy fellow
Weeds said the man, flowers said the child
God's own garden growing wild.

Helen Young

THE CHANGING OF THE SEASONS

When the summer sun begins to fade away,
And summer flowers have had their day.
When autumn sneaks in green and brown,
And treetop foliage flutters down.
When squirrels work frantically hiding food,
And birds split up from their fledgling brood.
When days start to shorten by minutes each end,
And on evening light to work in, you can no longer depend.
When the temperature drops each week by degrees,
And once again trousers cover sun bronzed knees.
When people dust off winter coats and shoes,
And evening activities are restricted to a snooze.
When TV pages of newspapers are read,
And by 10 o'clock you're ready for bed.
When lawns only need cutting once a fortnight,
And it's difficult to get the garden to look right.
When dried out flower beds are swilled with rain,
And sandy soil looks like earth again.
When people and animals prepare for the change,
And thick winter clothing when first put on feels strange.
As summer sun changes to autumn breeze,
And the leaves are rustling around the trees.
We know that these are changing times,
As nature reveals to us the signs
Of the changing of the seasons year after year,
But it's still a thing that brings me cheer.
Every season's change I hope I'll see,
Because then the gift of life will still be with me.
And at every change I have good reason,
To love the changing of the season.

David Ford

AUTUMN

As the dawn of the day begins to unfurl
The damp grey mist seems to drift and swirl,
It hangs in the hollow and clings to the river,
The spider's web seems to sparkle and shimmer.

As the sun begins to filter through
It bathes the leaves in a golden hue,
As they wither, they gently drift and fall,
The trees begin to look gaunt and tall.

A carpet of leaves now covers the ground,
Red, yellow and gold can all be found.
Soon there will be a sharp nip in the air
Then the plants and trees will be naked and bare.

The moorland hills once covered with heather
Are dark and blackened by the chill autumn weather.
Streams that flowed gently at an idle pace
Start to rush through valleys as if in a race.

Our stores are now full of fruit and grain,
Only bare trees and fields of stubble remain.
Squirrels have gathered in their winter stores,
Whilst we settle by our fires with tightly closed doors.

Muriel E Read

CHANGE

January stands silent still, holding the promise of change
   we hope it will fulfil.
February can fool us, lead us astray with early buds
   breaking through on a winter's day.
March moves forward with a whirling gust, around daffodils
   that show a tall and upward thrust.
April an ocean of lightest green, young cool and so serene.
May shouts its entrance with bursting bloom, of pink and white
   that fall far too soon.
June, July stately, now that Nature is full fledged,
   takes us to the very edge, of
August the odd one out, it's inconsistent changeable
   without a doubt.
September, October for me a painful time, as all around
   moves towards a slow decline.
November things tidied up put away, damp misty mornings
   herald each new day.
December with blood-red berries bright among the trees
   waiting to be picked for days of fun and festivity.
This circle of life repeated again and again,
But now certainty questioned, will it always remain?

S E Spooner

OCTOBER TREES

Branches outstretched, touching a watery sky,
Changing into autumn garb, orange, gold and red.
The last green leaves dance to the music of the breeze,
Whispering a sad song to the dying year.

Lynn Brookes

AUTUMN LESSON

I sit beneath
    My tree again
the wheel of time
    has turned,
golden leaves are falling now
    for autumn has returned.

From buds
    to flowers
        to leaves
            to fruit
their story they have told,
from brown
    to green
        to copper, and
            finally, to gold.

Scarlett

Now at the height
    of crowning glory,
the culmination of their reign,
    they offer of their riches
That life may start again.

This is a higher lesson
    that few of us
have learned
    to let go
        and to offer
the treasures we have earned.

OH EARTH! OH EARTH!

A burning instead of beauty
Great and fair, now she is
Dried up like a faded leaf
She had a garment of diver's colours upon her
For with such robes the King's daughters
That were virgins apparelled
Today she has been defiled
They discover her secret parts
The inhabitants have brought her out of the chamber
And bolted the door after her
The planet earth has put ashes on her head
And rent her garments of diver's colours
And laid her hand on her head
And went crying
For we must needs die
As water split on the ground
Which cannot be gathered up again
We looked for peace but no good came
And for a time of health and behold trouble
The lion has roared who will not fear?

Ebenezer Essuman

A Spring Tonic

Wandering through the country lanes
I saw brown horses with long black manes!
I spotted a ewe, about to give birth,
I waited with baited breath, quietly.
The little lamb was born, was it a daughter or son?
I moved, to take the lane on the right.

Here, the hedge was alive with noise,
Cute little birds in their nests - mouths poised,
Waiting anxiously to be fed, I even
Saw fish sunbathing on their riverbed.
Slowly I walked along the riverbank,
Where the beautiful wildflowers stood rank.
I paused to catch my breath and
Marvelled at Mother Nature's wealth.

Up over the hill I rambled, where
Woolly lambs gambolled, and baby rabbits
Played at their burrows, while the earth
The farmer worked with the harrow.
I sipped the cool water, inhaled the air so pure and clean,
Wishing time would never end this scene.
Beauty, peace and health abound in the country
After all the winter ills - this surely is a bounty!

Maisie Roberts

God's Seasons

In winter time, when icy winds do blow,
With days so short, and nights so long,
The field is covered with frozen snow,
Flanked by trees, that stand so strong.

Their leaves have gone, now blown away,
Only branches now point to our heaven,
They will stand forlorn, as if to pray,
Till warm winds come down from heaven.

When spring arrives, with warm breezes,
And the daylight lengthens in the sky,
We soon forget all the winter sneezes,
When migrating birds, to this land fly.

Soon appear the buds and green leaves,
Followed by the blossoms on the trees.
Soon birds begin to nest in the eaves,
Others rear their young in your trees.

Soon summer comes with all your glory,
The days are long with glorious skies.
Warm summer evenings tell God's story,
Christ is your truth, Jesus never lies.

Then comes the harvest, He did send us,
The wheat and crops, men need to exist.
God gave them freely, as was our Jesus,
He died for all who cry out to Christ.

Autumn now returns, to remind us again,
Another year is now coming to its end.
Life is short, with suffering and pain,
So we need Christ Jesus, as our friend.

Fred Schofield

Winter-Logged

The woods are wet again
And you can safely bet
That branches brushed against
Will spitefully spit
Salvos of icy water
To trickle unerringly inside your collar.

The paths are tetchy too
And if your feet go from under
The bushes are only too glad
To coldly embrace your fall
And deposit their spare damp
On your elbows and seat.

The best hope's a bumptious wind
To shoo the clouds to the wings,
Bring on the sun to show off a bit
And shine the trees clean-green
(Not lime, not bottle, not emerald
But sparkling leaf-live green).

Then the insects taking cover
From the raindrop doodle-bugs
Would emerge with an all-clear buzz
And you'd hear birds busy discussing
What they fancied for a late lunch
Not, after all, rained-off.

Not a chance at the moment though
It's almost cold enough for snow
And the clouds hold the skies so freezily fogged
That the woods aren't just wet - they're winter-logged.

Dick Anstis

SPRING

Spring is here again at last,
The long cold winter is in the past.
Bulbs are showing their little green shoots,
As if to tell us they also have roots.
Daffodils are like the morning sunshine,
The snowdrops burst forth and say 'I'm fine.'
The lambs are skipping on new grassy slopes,
People smile again with joy and hopes.
Spring's a time for a new beginning,
Of happiness and laughter ringing.
So lift your head and enjoy the sun,
Smile everyone and have some fun.

Doreen Hadfield

SUMMER SAILS

Sparkling in the summer sunshine,
The sighing of the wind through the shrouds.
Is it God whispering to you on the breeze?
My world is beautiful! Why do you desecrate it so?
Catch the colours of the rainbow
In a drop of morning dew,
Misty covered cobwebs trembling and sparkling
In the morning light,
White clouds against a deep blue sky.
These are treasures beyond compare.
Why don't you stop, and stand, and stare!
He created all this, and more for you,
Just open your heart and mind
And you will see!

Fredrick Caxton Holt

HAVE YOU OVERLOOKED ANYTHING TODAY?

The sensation of wind, blowing through your hair,
lifting, rearranging each strand as it passes flowingly by.
Birds gracing the sky with their beautiful displays of flight
and motion, even chirps, whistles, like love songs from
one bird to another, from their little hearts.
The shear greatness of a tree swaying to and fro in the wind,
leaves turning, twisting, giving off a tremendous rustling sound.
Sometimes yielding to this effect some leaves tumble to the ground,
released from their branch of life once more.
Oh! The vastness of the sky, the warmth of the sun, the freshness
of the very air.
To love and be loved in return.
All this is truly magnificent, have you overlooked anything today?

Pablo Hamill Magee

THE SNOWDROP

When dark December's dreary days have flown
And January's sleet and snow are gone,
The 'fair maid of February' does appear,
The snowdrop, harbinger of spring each year;
She in her pure and modest mantle clad,
Uplifts our spirits, bids our hearts be glad,
Tells us that winter's chills will bite no more,
When warmer days emerge from Nature's store.

Edward Farren

SPRINGTIME

Spring is here, the birds are singing -
Of the new season it is bringing.
Life to trees, buds are sprouting
Children playing, laughing, shouting -
Of a new day clean and crisp.
Watching the fledglings taking the risk -
To fly for the first time, unaided by mum.
Will it fly or drop into a waiting cat's tum?

Leaves unfold, stretching with glee
Forming strange patterns upon the tree
Blossom like confetti on the bough.
New life beginning in the woodland now
Flowers popping their heads above ground.
Coming up, surfacing without a sound,
Petals unfolding, their scent divine.
So let's savour it all for another time.

S Askew

THE SKY

As I walk down the road
with both children holding onto me,
I look above to see the clouds in the sky.
They're so bubbly, and so white.
The sky is so blue.
The sun is shining in my eyes
And it reminds me of my hometown
Where I was born, which is called Liverpool.
It made me smile as the birds sung
And all I can say is
I'm so glad to be here and to be alive.

Bonnie M Frier

1998, Mum's Summer Blues

We waited for spring, but it never came,
We looked for summer, but that was in vain,
For August the sun popped in and out,
Furiously hot in small doses, but loved,
Between the sun so cold, windy and glum,
And *wet*.

By the end of August rain again and humidity,
Forecasters admitted summer failed to come,
There was to be no Indian summer as we
    hoped, but straight into autumn.
                              Ah me!
We hope they are wrong.

M M Watson

WINTER

Winter - season of snow and Christmas trees,
Winter - the shouts of children as they play,
Winter - rosy cheeks and friends to tease,
Winter, enchantment every day.

The snow falls silently before we wake,
A carpet of white, no blemish in sight,
And when we rise we see the frozen lake,
Wonder - has this happened in just one night?

How the children love to roll about,
Their snow-filled boots, their happy faces,
When in for tea, we're left in no doubt,
They can't wait to go back, resume their races.

Christmas Eve, - the sound of bells ringing,
Magic in the air, the feel of peace,
And all around is the age-old singing
Of carols, wonder of words that never cease.

Christmases past were still exciting,
Although the toys were simple and few,
But today the spirit is less inviting,
Children expect expensive gifts too.

But all in all, winter is still a wonder,
Curtains drawn, chestnuts on the fire,
Turkey, mince pies, cake for all to plunder,
And the joy we feel listening to the choir.

Christmas Eve - time of expectation,
Stockings for Father Christmas to fill,
Bringing toys to feed children's imagination,
Something for every Jack and Jill.

But still my family remembers for sure,
The first Christmas which brought a life so pure.

Jill Silverman

THE WONDERS OF THE MAKER

Spring - summer - autumn - winter,
Four seasons of the year repeating,
Each one with a special greeting.

Springtime in all its splendour,
Filling earth and skies aglow.
Summertime, most days sunny and warm,
And beautiful evening sunsets show.
Autumn, my favourite,
Glory of God's golden year, still here,
Midst tumbling leaves laced in colours bright.
      What a beautiful sight.
Winter next, cosy and warm,
With fires alight.
Praise to the Maker, God the Creator.

Madeline Green

LAST SUMMER

Strawberries and cream tease the palette,
Unfurled leaves green with innocence
Taste the new-born day.
Swirling lawn skirts the old pavilion,
Ice cream cumulous keeps the sun at bay.

Slice and chip tactics test the metal,
Subtle lob overheads
Drive the opposition wild.
Dessert dish served in desperation
Saves the day, but only for a while.

A peach of a shot seals the final victory,
Game, set and match,
The home team wins at last.
Spectators with their Sunday feast completed
Saunter through the shadows of the past.

Is that the roar of generous applause?
The thwack of tennis balls and doubtful calls?
Is that the west wind in the coppice sighing?
No, just the sound of all those summers dying.

Sandra Davies

CYCLE OF THE SEASONS

As winter envelops the autumn,
And covers its leaves with snow,
Hiding the nuts and the berries,
All but those buried below -
So, winter is humorously hustled
When the sun champions the spring
And, smilingly backed by the breezes,
Starts cleaning up everything.

Then summer comes smiling and laughing,
Promoting the sun to first place,
And decking the gardens with flowers,
Cajoling the birds, us, to grace
With a chorus of songs just to cheer us,
And bring us out, dancing with glee,
Sporting our bright summer dresses,
To sit in the sun for our tea.

Too soon the clouds, feeling jealous,
Roll by to hide the sun's face,
Calling the cold wind and weather,
And driving the rain on apace:
Too soon they buffet in autumn,
Robbing the sun of its charm;
Tho' it dresses its leaves in bright colours,
It sends storm winds to scurry them down.

Thus, winter envelops the autumn,
Holding tightly with fingers so cold,
Then, again, begins the same cycle,
As Nature's seasons begin to unfold.

Bee Wickens

CLOAKS OF GREEN

Autumn fires their branches with hues of red and gold,
Dressed them in gowns of flame cloaks so bright and bold.

Winter with its cold stark light looks down upon the land,
They shed their cloaks of red and gold.
Like skeletons they stand,
Their branches reaching outwards,
Bony fingers on a hand.

Cold winds bring the snowfall silently at night,
Bony fingers with diamonds shimmer
A gift of pale moonlight.
Like ghosts they stand all winter long in gowns of virgin white.

Springtime brings its soft warm rain,
Washes gowns of white away.
Fingers once adorned with diamonds now emeralds display,
And in branches cloaked once more in green the gentle breezes play.

M Lloyd

FEBRUARY PINIONS

The birds are singing today.
Why today?
A damp grey grizzle day indistinguishable
(at least to me)
from yesterday, the day before,
a dozen days or more in recent weeks.
The thrush - well, he's been yelling
his head off since Christmas:
but great tit and dunnock
tip-tap and tweedle-wheedle
While talkative starlings hold a conference.
Memory and the calendar tell me
there'll be a great uprising soon:
they know - just know.
In former years I've often wondered how;
not now.
I apprehend the source from which
their knowledge springs -
but I have no wings.

J Allison

The Horse Chestnut Tree

I'm a magnificent horse chestnut tree,
In spring a wondrous sight to see.
My blossoms like candles in the sky,
Give pleasure to all who pass me by.

Summer with its warming sun,
The formation of my fruits begun.
My leaves take on a darker shade,
A cooling shelter they have made.

Autumn is the time I fear,
It's a bad time for me each year.
Boys with sticks my body beat,
To knock down fruit they cannot eat.

When winter comes my frame is bare,
With bruises and scratches everywhere.
Along comes spring to ease my pain,
Then the cycle must start again.

Mick Moyce

It's Not The Same Without The Raspberry Ripple

I do not care for an autumnal pallet,
But winter I find is harsh and bleak,
And spring can keep its host of daffodils,
It's of the summer I wish to speak,
Not of the warmth of a blistering sun,
Or a roam across an evening shore,
Walking hand in hand with the one I love, no,
My pleasures are far more pure.
I love the way my tongue tingles,
The way my lips become cold and numb,
Each varying delicious texture,
Now that's my idea of fun.
I bow to all your tempting flavours,
I delight in the lost childhood which you extract from me,
And gaze in awe at your flawless dimensions,
Raised in my hand for all to see.
For me you are the epitome of summer,
Exhibited blatantly, not hidden, no riddle,
So pay homage to the humble ice cream cone,
For summer's not the same without the raspberry ripple.

Skye Taylor

CHANGING SEASONS

How do I see the seasons change?
From spring to summer, autumn and winter.
The latter may be combined as one.
As I walk through a graveyard
some trees may be left bare by autumn,
unprepared for winter's terrible tales!
Shall I just say it all boils down to -
the approach of Christmas!
Or of nostalgic poachers stealing from Mother Nature?
Carpeting the ground with leaves in autumn,
can only new flowers blossom in spring.
One can then only think of new spring lambs being born.
Like my mother's love of Christmas roses,
pure white, sparkling and bright!
Against many gravestones,
sometimes upright, round-shaped
or even cross-shaped.
Entangled with holly with red berries,
most tied with red ribbons.
Most memories are precious at Christmas,
therefore the cosiness of the Christmas.
Round laurel takes presents over mantelpieces,
front doors!
As most people prefer the cosiness of the warm coal fire,
leaving winter raging outside.
Only the four seasons remain to be seen!

Lynda Margaret Firth

THE FALL

Strong and sturdy stand the trees,
As autumn winds through branches sough -
Murmuring low they coax and tease
The golden leaves from every bough.

They softly fall to hardened ground
And protected lie 'neath trees' vast girth -
Till changing wind disturbs the mound -
And scatters them o'er all the earth.

The now bare arms of trees once proud
Are outstretched helplessly in space -
Their fruits the fens and fields enshroud,
Blown far away from strong embrace.

The fall of Man is as the leaves -
When Satan's low and murmuring sound -
Coaxes him till he believes
That joy of life is in him found.

Lord Jesus is the Tree of Life,
His arms outstretched to lift and Save
Fallen man from Satan's strife
And devious methods to deprave.

Strong and powerful is Our Tree,
The Tree of Life - Our Saviour,
To Him we humbly bow the knee,
And pray for guidance in behaviour.

The wind of change God soothes, becalms,
For Man the Path of Life He'll pave
And embrace him in His loving arms,
For eternity his soul to Save.

Marian Curtis Jones

AUTUMN LOVE

The flowers decay
But our love is just beginning to grow

The sun diminishes
But our bodies glow with warmth

The winds blow
But we cling to one another

The rain pours
But we have each other for shelter

The days darken
But out love is light.

Tahira

ROCKY MOUNTAIN MEMORIES
(The bugling elks of Jackson Hole)

I can recall that autumnal sound
Whenever I close my eyes and travel
In my mind, to that paradise across the sea
Where the elk graze the golden grass of late summer
And the early migrant geese-filled evenings glow in
Jackson Hole in the Rocky Mountains, and my memory
Curious bobcats, wolves and grizzly bears come to witness
The ritual push of war of the twelve-point antlers
Leading to the victor mating and the start of bugling shrills
Tension of the yellowy rutting season, rising, rising
Crescending as the triumphant bull trumpets his magnificence
Broadcasting his valour to the universe in disjointed wails.

>The bugling days of autumn -
>Splendour in the grass
>Everlasting music of season
>Nothing can surpass.

P R McDonald

AUTUMN

When the trees are disrobing and throwing their foliage around,
When the rime on the meadow makes patterns of translucent hue,
When the Michaelmas daisies are battling their way through the mound
Of leaves, when the sky is despondent and cobwebs are
    glistening with dew.
When the seas are in turmoil and flotsam is strewn on the shore,
When fires create patterns on curtains drawn mid-afternoon,
When the sun tries to warm but only has power to draw
The mist, slowly creeping to envelop the landscape with gloom.
When the 'water' sign Scorpio is sharing the 'fire' Sagittarius,
When the justice of Pluto and wisdom of Jupiter rules,
When the 'Archer' outspoken is dualled with 'Scorpion' nefarious
And deep; as a stream swiftly flowing descends to dark
    fathomless pools.
When the bells ring their changes and challenge the wars of futility,
When the Services gather and battles are relived anew,
When two minutes silence is given to show the humility
We feel; when the poppies cascade and the many remember the few.
When unwilling victims are struck down by virus infections,
When people are muffled and snuffling about in their woe,
When buses are run with a chaotic loss of connections
With trains; when commuters are harassed by 'cancelled'
    or at best 'go-slow'.
When the countryside's dreary and animals huddle together,
When gardens are barren of colour and birds rarely sing,
When the main conversation's predicting the state of the weather
To come; and consoling ourselves that it's one season nearer to spring.
When the fields, tilled and desolate tell us that winter approaches,
When the hedgerows are silent and minus all signs of creation,
When the chill seeks the helpless; despair not and bear no reproaches
For November's the month of the phoenix - the regeneration.

Pam Owers

SUMMERTIME SPECIAL

The summertime special is my caravan
Going to places whenever I can
Starting in June as the warmth comes through
There's nothing in the world that you cannot do
A nice steady ramble in the countryside
The sun on your back a smile so wide
Happiness abounds you feel so good
Summertime at last you knew you would
Time to move on down to the coast
It's getting hotter now July's your host
The caravan site is right on the beach
Nothing seems to be out of reach
A promenade walk a nice sea breeze
Much better than winter you'll know you won't freeze
You sit by your van and look out to sea
What a wonderful sunset something that's free
It's getting so hot there's a sea fret about
And it's oh so eerie when you hear someone shout
It takes a while for it to move away
But when it does it's a beautiful day
Time to move on the New Forest we'll go
August is here it's still hot you know
You can't beat a summer with plenty of sun
There's something for all with plenty of fun
See the wild horses running around
Things to see lots to be found
Warm hazy days a stroll in the wood
See nature at its best you know you should
It's coming to a close as autumn draws near
But the summertime special is oh so dear.

T G Porter

AVENUE, AUTUMN

Wild, red rage of sunset turning,
Sad, autumnal bonfires burning,
Stubbed-out ends of aspirations,
Wasted embers, spirit-yearning.

Stars through naked branches sifting,
Bygone lives like flotsam drifting,
Lees of empty expectations,
Lonely song of earth uplifting.

Silent dreams in dusk unfurling,
Moon - her soft beams headlong hurling,
Sombre twilight ruminations,
Soul, like incense, heavenward curling.

Falling leaf in spiral wending,
Earthbound journey never-ending,
Final, half-formed meditations,
Spirits of the past ascending.

S H Smith

CHANGING SEASONS OF THE HEART

Spring, First love, and gentle showers,
Interspersed with sun-ripe hours.
Arm-in-arm, we watch the lambs
Skipping round their doting dams.

Summer. Love grows ever stronger,
Musk scents the days, night light lasts longer.
Heart on beating heart we lie
'Neath Venus and her starry eye.

Autumn. There's no use pretending.
Our love is near its tearful ending.
Little joy, red mists of pain.
Outside, a near hurricane!

Winter, and the heart grows chill.
Love's out of sight, the times bode ill.
A card from you! A Christmas dove
Heralding rebirth of love.

Elizabeth Mark

SILVER THREADS

Season of silver threads 'mongst the laburnum leaves.
Sparkling dewdrops nestling on night-enshrouded lawn.
Delicate lacy lingerie floating faintly on wings of air,
Creating an air of peace to a bright new dawn.
A web woven so fine, so delicate to touch,
Like the touch of a young man's fondest love.
A very quiet beauty that reveals wisdom in its path
For who could create such a perfect picture?
Just think and look to the heavens above.

Betty Foot

CHANGING SEASONS

As I look out from my window
And watch the passing seasons
I'm filled with awe and wonder
And think of all the reasons

Why? First we have the springtime,
So fresh, so new, so green.
All on Earth awakens
Bringing hope where gloom has been.

Along comes summer, warm and bright
With flowers of every hue.
The world seems oh so beautiful,
And our hearts are filled anew.

When autumn comes, the world is filled
With so much warmth and cheer.
Leaves from the trees make a carpet of gold,
What a lovely time of year.

Last but not least is the winter
With its storms, ice and snow.
But as we snuggle up indoors,
We are filled with a special glow.

If I had picked my favourite
I think I would choose the Fall,
But each has its own fascination,
Let's agree, we of course love them all.

Babe Morgan

SUMMER ON THE FOYLE

I love the light from the west
The light that seems to hang
In the sky for hours.
The planes fly low over the Lough
On sycamore wings,
And on cloudy summer days
The wind will always blow
Soft, silver sheets of rain
To wrap me in.
I love the wind.
So this is what it is to feel content.

Debbie Caulfield

DISTORTED IMAGES ON A WINDSWEPT AFTERNOON

Fantastical imagery
And shadowy spectres
Concealed in a mesh
Of mental trickery
Haunting unattainable
Dispersed in the wind
Darting through light and shade
Deceptive like chameleons
Extinguished by the fading light.

Jim Nicholas

THE SEA AND THE SEASONS

The waves come rolling in, up onto the shore,
Laughing children jump over them, shouting for more.
The watchful eyes of the parents, become veiled with memory,
Of when they themselves as toddlers played beside the sea.
Looking in rock pools for crabs, shells, and fish.
Days then were endless, and all you could wish.
So passes sweet summer in warm balmy days,
The sand and the castles that shimmer in the haze.
Comes autumn now, morning mists, shorter days, swift the tide flows,
The children still come to play on the beach, now dressed
                                                            in warmer clothes.
Then winter comes, the beach now deserted, and so very bleak,
The sea now pounds the solitary shore, gulls wheel high above
                                                            and shriek.
Against the rocks and the bare grey cliffs,
Hangs a ghostly fog that scarcely lifts.
Vengeful winds, driving all before it, ships and man,
Longing to be back in safe harbour again.
From a cottage on the cliffs above, beams a strong welcoming light,
To the homecoming sailor, a heart-warming sight.
The storm is now over, wind drops to a sigh, from a roar,
And the waves are at peace now, as they lap the shore
And folks in their houses, feel safe, as they may,
They smile in the knowledge that spring is on the way
And the sea that is grey now, soon will turn blue.
The sea and the seasons, old pleasures to renew.

Eileen Cuddy Buckley

HELLO WINTER!

A blanket of snow makes everything
Look so clean and bright.
Yes the winter months can be
Quite a remarkable sight!
Morning frost that sparkle sending,
A penetrating chill in the air.
Leaving mosaic designs everywhere,
But never two the same to compare!

Even though the sun filters through,
Sometimes mustering up strength,
But although the days are shorter now,
Nights draw in at great lengths.
With gusting strong winds that
Whip up everything in sight,
Causing driving rain to penetrate,
So keeping warm and dry is a fright!

When the mists come rolling in, spooky
And dangerous for you're unseen,
But when it lifts to reveal the world,
There's no evidence where it has been.
Thunder and lightning rips across the sky,
Shouting its torment with rage.
The fear of a trail of devastation,
Then floodwaters beat the barricades!

Even though there's beauty in all seasons,
There's the element of struggle too,
Adding to the magic and mystery of life,
How you cope with it, makes you!

Ann Beard

TIME'S FRIEND

As winter slowly turns to spring
And all that was frozen lives once more
Deep inside my heart summer still is born
I wonder, yet know that your love still grows
Just as the trees spring into life
And nature rules once more

As summer resumes over the throne of glory
And reminds life that as gentle he can be
He can yet still be cruel to all who do not respect
I see, I remember clearly all that I once was
As dust blows and then falls
All that is, will be again

Autumn knows no time and no limit,
And before summer has a chance to grow, rain falls
At first a fresh reminder to life, as if life could forget
But too soon a cold reminder of what is to come
It seems to all autumn has won
But as all, all can be so wrong

Winter freezes all and lays patiently for time
I await your love that has long since passed away
I too am frozen awaiting a chance to join you
Time is my friend and the seasons my days
But I too know that soon
You shall join me and I shall join you.

J C Walters

WINTERS LONG AGO

I remember Christmas at my granny's long ago
when the Earth was covered with ice and snow.
We had no electricity and read by candlelight,
if you thought that we'd be happy, of course you'd be right.

We did not have television or have video games,
the food that we ate was just wholesome and plain
an orange and apple was all Santa brought
he didn't bring computer or adidas shorts.

But we did have the wireless
and we laughed at ITM
and Dick Barton Special Agent
to us was a star.

We ate figgy pudding and good old spotted dick
and we sang Christmas carols
while my dad tapped his stick.

He played the mouth organ
as he rocked in his chair
and we played cat's cradle.
Oh I wished you'd been there.

When my dad carved the turkey
and we all bowed our heads
oh how happy we felt
that winter's night in our beds

Amy Cornes Torr

A Walk In The Woods

I love to walk in the woods
on the first fine day of spring.
The whispering of the trees,
the busy birds on the wing.

The misty carpet of bluebells,
breathing nostalgic scent
of first spring days long past,
of other years long spent.

I love to walk in the woods
on the first fine day of spring
and see the sun filtering through
and hear the songbirds sing.

The fresh green leaves, their tale
to tell, that life has just begun,
and very soon they will enjoy
the warmth of summer sun.

When I walk in the woods I know
that life will spring anew
for trees and birds and flowers,
my heart will sing so, too.

Rozetta Pate

SNOWDROPS

Pretty snowdrops in a cluster
Rays of sunshine light your lustre.
Drooping heads reflect my mood
In the shadows of the wood,
With creeping ivy everywhere
When up you spring, here and there.
Splashes of white amongst the green
The leafless trees in hazy dream.
Then as I pass, I stop to gaze
And ponder at this woodland maze.
A wonderland within the trees
Swaying gently in the breeze:
I lift your little head serene
But leave you, in your tranquil scene.

Jill Barker

WINTER
THE LAST CROP

The lightning-split oak
Stands proud and true.
Once part of the forest
Now one of a few.

Carved on its trunk
Love-hearts, dates and names.
Children have climbed
Whilst playing their games.

Eighty years standing
Now weathered and worn.
The last crop of acorns
From this tree will be borne.

For a winter is coming
A winter so bad.
The old oak will be fallen,
Gone, the life that it had.

Mark Himlin

AUTUMN

Autumn is the time of year
when the corn is cut and threshed.
The farmers work so very hard
to get the harvest in.
Apples red and rosy hanging from the trees,
pears and plums swaying in the autumn breeze.
Hedgerows heavily laden with blackberries,
hips and haws.
Beech nuts, acorns falling to the floor.
Softly leaves are falling burgundy, orange
and red.
Twirling past my window as I watch them
from my bed.
Autumn brings the mist and dew
silver cobwebs, holly too.

Callum Tweed (9)

SPRING COLOURS

Spring's variety of flora
that robes the land each year,
subdues into a vernal baize
as the summer's heat draws near.

The brightest hues pervade each spring
and precede the darker leaf;
with colourful abundance
so brilliant, yet so brief.

Such magnificence and splendour
seem engendered of a charm,
where existence will be cherished
within a sea of calm.

Yet, fading glows of floral growth
convey nostalgia to the scene,
as life's first plumage slowly softens:
The rainbow turns to sultry green.

So exotic and ethereal
as of another clime,
where beauty and nostalgia
can flourish and combine.

Susan Turner

THE SNOWDROP
(Dedicated to Sarjini Vamblie)

The snowdrop is a hardy flower
Although it is so small, it shows a lot of power
To push its way through hard frosty earth
To show the world God's creation worth
Such a tiny snow-white flower, is seen
Amongst the plants, trees and even evergreens
It braves itself against frost and snow
To beautify the woods as everybody knows
I picked a little snowdrop one day
A little flower of springtime they say
I looked at it carefully, wandering how was it made
But God's creations are full of wonderful things, is said
I likened it as a nurse I know, she is so petite
Always does her work well, and she is nice and neat
She works looking after the old and infirm
And she is gentle and kind, of this I confirm,
So carry on your good work, 'Sarojini' with the old
Dedicated to your nursing profession, and never cold.

R T Owen

ALL THIS

Lovely greens of spring,
Such high spirits bring,
As hard nature tries
And life multiplies.

Lovely shades of summer,
How could I wish for more?
Not even in a dream
Could I add to the store.

Hazel Cullis

MOTHER EARTH

Her beauty is admired
from those in space.
The sun circles round her
with a smile on his face.
She allows us to live with her,
provides for our needs,
but what do we give her
in return for her deeds?
Man destroys vegetation,
blows up her seas,
Pollutes her land, plus the air
that she breathes.
'Fighting', 'destruction',
is all we return.
How stupid we are,
will we never learn?
What we give out
we will get in return.

Maureen Nash

SUMMER'S SADNESS

These are the days I love the best,
When all the fields seem full of rest,
When early morning's breath nips at my face,
And late summer's wafting perfume's here
In this quiet place.

Now, here and there, a breath of warm breeze comes,
Late of the April days.
The insect in the hedge still hums,
As autumn sheds her rays.

Birds chirp in hazel hedges hung with dew,
(A sadder note, for summer's nearly over),
I stand and see a nearby view of hanging roses,
Or some late-bud, browning clover.

The drone of aircraft fades, to leave a peaceful sound
A scythe somewhere whistles past the ground,
And where the lynch-gate swings, a blackbird sings,
Filling the freshened sky, with bittersweet and haunting cry,
My heart is gladdened by it all,
These wistful days in autumn - fall . . .

Jane Mills

NATURE'S TREASURES

Gone are all the lazy days
Carpets of flowers in a summer haze
The refreshing music of a garden fountain
Sun and shadows on yonder mountain

It's autumn now - carpets of gold
Although the sun shines it is rather cold
The squirrels are busy collecting nuts
For when there's snow and the icy wind cuts

The trees are bare and the robins sing
The summer birds gone - all on the wing
Hedgehogs and tortoises all fast asleep
Tucked away safely, not even a peep

The days are getting longer now
Little buds bursting on every bough
Colour returns, violet and gold
Green and yellow and blue to behold

Soon the swallows will be here
Another summer, another year
Every season has its pleasures
Nature reveals its hidden treasures

Can one be better than the rest?
And can you say which one is best?
Each season's charm is all its own
God's wonders in them all are shown

__Josephine Western__

GOD'S GIFT OF LOVE

This is the yellow time
Of forsythia, daffodils and budding crocus dancing on the
    fresh spring breeze
And proud narcissus gazing down
Upon clumps of prim, shy snowdrops peeping beneath the trees.
This is the blue time, when grape hyacinths raise their
    cone-shaped heads.
Ragwort, Honesty and mauve button forget-me-nots cover
    the flower beds
The time for hyacinths of pink and white opening to the warming sun.
The flowers of Holland, pointing sentinels, show their faces.
When the warming rays touch everyone.
The tulip blossomed magnolias grace the twisted branches
    with profusion
And swelling buds of apple green, follow their shoots,
bursting visually from the branches of the sycamore boughs
Pale pink horse chestnuts and powdery catkins of the pussy willows
Drooping down as if to touch the backs of browsing cows
When white pear blossoms mix with deeper cherry petals on
    the quickening breeze.
This is the time of scented roses, suspended from their thorn-tipped
    branches overhead.
To reach the pointed fingers of the blue delphiniums,
    reaching from their flowery beds
And coy wide-eyed violas and pansies smiling from borders
    of summer roses.
Where the sweet fresh perfume of camomile and pinks caress
    our noses,
With aromas of summer spent.
God's bright canopy of love that is heaven sent.

Rev Harry Rolfe

CHANGING SEASONS

Of all the seasons that England brings
Arrives yet again the glorious spring
When the early sunbeams brightly shine through
Clearing the grey clouds away, to shades of blue

When the swarthy moods of the mist disappears
Blackbirds sing out their notes of cheers
Noisy rattle sounds like an alarm, high then low
As the mistle thrush sits listening on a tree bough

Showing heavy dark spots on her creamy breast
Near where sparrows are resting on their well-built nest
The thrush joins the blackbirds, calling out a chattering praise
Repeating three or four notes, and a brief whistling phrase

Echoes through the woodlands, where such sweetness sounds
Where lilac and lime of contrasts blossom on the tree around
When in apple blossom time, bluebells are gathered
As the gentle breeze blows the orchards, where nature is covered

Then Mother Nature is at work, to show God's creation
Through His wondrous works, when we see with admiration
As daffodils bloom out showing bright yellow faces
Until, tulips are seen around flower beds with fragrances and graces

Through the warmth of the days, birds fly through the air
Blue-throats are heard, with soft variety notes that are rare
Through the wonders of nature, as birds mate and multiply
Bringing more joyfulness, throughout the wondrous sky

Until the sunset draws and goes down, and twilight draws near
Rich, remarkable notes of nightingales calls out so clear
But, God knows about the mysteries, when the dusk gets darker
For He watches over all, through His great Might and Power

When the days dance away, through the changing seasons
While autumn is still bright, whenever the sunray glistens.

Jean P McGovern

SPRINGTIME

Through the warm air, on the first month of spring
Rabbits are around the fields, jumping and hopping
Birds fly from the east heading towards the south and west
Soon they will carry straw and twigs in their beaks to build their nest

As we listen to their joyful notes singing merrily
Where Mother Nature spreads out God's nature and beauty
Where daffodils bloom out, and are seen all around
Through all God's creation where loveliness is found

Where trees seem to whisper, as the gentle breeze blows
As leaves sway to and fro, where a colourful scene shows
When the sun smiles down, and everything looks bright
Through God's powerful works, and His shining light

When springtime is here and Easter approaches
Children getting excited for the Milk Tray eggs
As the preparations go on at the village church hall
More merriment is heard, with the feasting on this festival

How wonderful to know that Jesus' good Spirit lives on
Who made everything in the springtime, and each season
Especially when we see birds fly through the air
And rabbits hop in and out of their burrows without a care

Kathleen Spilsbury

THE QUIET MAN

When the sun is rising in the east and the world's eye is opened
When flowers yawn 'neath the dewy dawn before the first word's spoken,
'Tis then you'll see the quiet man tread softly on his way
Along the paths of yesteryear as the two dogs bound in play.

When the sun is sinking in the west and all is bathed red-gold,
When the moon is high in the starlit sky and the dragonfly grow old,
'Tis then you'll see the quiet man, the two dogs by his side
Tread the paths of solitude, the narrow and the wide.

When the tempest blows and the wind rides high, across
                                            the storm-lashed sea,
When the snow lies deep and the ground's asleep,
                                            beneath the wint'ry lea,
'Tis then you'll see the quiet man, wend his way no less
With Judy there to check the snare and run awhile with Bess.

When the sunshine bathes the summer fields and the broom's
                                            a joyous yellow,
Or when Autumn gold, turns new to old and the misty
                                            meadow's mellow,
When the hedgerow's sweet and the deer can eat their fill
                                            from saplings new
'Tis then you'll see the quiet man, tread dawn and dusk and dew.

The quiet man can see the hand of God, in all things made
In freedom walks, no doors or locks, to bar the paths he's laid.
He'll sit a while, or stand a while, at one with nature's plan
Then call the two dogs to his side - on walks, the quiet man.

Alison Forbes

TRUE LOVE

Every time I see you smile
My heart does a flutter
With the feeling of a new beguile
Thought of you encourages my adrenaline matter
When I touch your tranquil hand
You respond with tender fingers
I earnestly surrender my caring soul like a band
Of solemn yet full of joy church-ringers
Peeling out our song of love
As a white-necked grey flying dove
Hovers to feast its eyes upon we two
From the heavens above so blue
We nestle divinely in each other's arms
Filled with peace and tranquility and everlasting calm

Alma Montgomery Frank

WONDERFUL THING IS SPRING

Wonderful thing is spring with new life beginning
The trees that begin to clothe with leaves that are green
Animals that come out to stretch and play after a winter's sleep
The flowers that blossom with wonderful colours that shower the land
All Nature awakes with the warmth of the sun
Wonderful thing is spring.

C J Walls

LIFE'S SEASONS

As I looked at the leaves on the hedgerows
Coloured brown, red, yellow, and gold,
It reminded me of our life's autumn
Which we sometimes call, 'Growing old'

As I thought of the springtime of childhood
Where all is young, tender and gay
Then the fresh bright green leaves of the hedgerows
Spoke to me of children at play

In the summer when bright flowers all blossom
The earliest fruit are then seen
This is true of the men and the women
Whose children now play on the green

The winter is a time of preparing
With the promise of things to come
We are waiting for the bulbs to open
Preparing for babes to be born

And as I think of all of life's seasons
The promises I find are clear
That one spring, summer, autumn and winter
Will lead on to another year

God has promised the seasons will not end
And His promises are all true
His promise of an everlasting life
Gives life's seasons a brighter hue

So I'll thank Him for all His promises
For the seed-time, harvest and rest
And I'll praise Him for all His love to me
For He makes life's seasons the best

P Rock

A Day To Remember

A sea of daisies
   with ponies
      grazing in the sun.
   Green grasses
     a calm breeze
       at ease
         with nature.
A game of cricket
  paced and steady
heady with the smell
      of new-mown hay.
   A summer's day
  strawberries and cream.
    A cool
      glass of wine
        divine.
Oh to be lost
  in this time.

C Webb

BEGONE THE WINTER

Cease! Oh cease! You black wind of depression.
Or, with your force, carry off those mists of grey.
Please to make a single, small, concession . . .
And, let the sun shine through . . . a single ray.

That we may see that, soon will follow on . . .
A drear, dull, winter soon will say farewell.
That sorrow, sadness flees, will soon be gone.
Then we at rest, in summer's green-clad dell.

Brenda Robson-Eifler

CHANGING SEASONS

Autumn dawns transforming the countryside,
Golden the field, brown the bracken, purple the ling,
Lending beauty to the season tide,
Summer bloom flown - like a bird on the wing.

Golden the field, brown the bracken, purple the ling,
Verdant green given way to flamboyant hue,
Summer bloom flown - like a bird on the wing,
Russet the leaf, bud of youth dew.

Verdant green given way to flamboyant hue,
Lush mellow fruit - the orchard's crown,
Russet the leaf, bud of youth dew,
Resplendent the moorland, clad in purple gown.

Lush mellow fruit - the orchard's crown,
Grains' golden crop, yields to the reaper,
Resplendent the moorland clad in purple gown,
Mingled ochre with tinges deeper.

Grains' golden crop, yields to the reaper,
The harvest secure in the winter store,
Mingled ochre with tinges deeper,
The migrant wings to a distant shore.

The harvest secure in the winter store
As come flurrying flakes of snow,
The migrant wings to a distant shore,
Carried on winds, that do blustery blow.

As come flurrying flakes of snow
Lending beauty to the seasontide -
Carried on winds that do blustery blow
Winter dawns transforming the countryside

Catherine J MacKenzie

SUMMER

Summer has come with all its delights;
Mother nature has brought wondrous colours so bright,
Buttercups and daisies on a carpet of green,
Snowy-white petals and yellow supreme.

Honeysuckle and rose in hedgerow a'nesting;
Aster and pansy in borders a'resting.
Phlox and wallflower, a kaleidoscope of colour,
Blooms of all kinds for us to discover.

The shrubbery too, magnolia, clematis,
Give us a view of splendour with gladness.
Lilac and cherry, blossoms galore,
Sweet smelling fragrance and lots more.

An umbrella of leaves; red, green and gold,
What a beauteous sight for all to behold.
Chaffinch and thrush, singing on high,
As swallows are gliding way up in the sky.

And down in a meadow on a lovely sunny day,
Field mice and rabbits are happy at play.
Even the streams are subjects of wonder,
Due to the presence of another summer.

William Stannard

AUTUMN

Imperceptibly, the mist arrives,
Heralding a change, a new season -
But follows up with riotous hues,
Glaring and bold, nature's last flourish.

Autumn for me is a beginning, not an end.
A time for introspection and prayer.
A loving, fun time, but with its sadness,
As slowly the leaves begin to fall.

The glistening red berries are sought after,
Fought over by birds that see the time
Of plenty, autumn's cornucopia soon over
To be followed by winter's shortage.

Some animals busy themselves storing,
Some looking for a place to sleep -
While others are brought to winter quarters
Made secure against the freezing blasts.

The sun will shine warmly one last time
Giving the hope needed for his return,
After a cold season of darkness and depression
That all is well and all ends well.

Gabrielle Hopkins

AUTUMN

As the leaves turn from
lively green to warm brown
and the harsh bright light
that invades my eyelids
far too early
turns into the comforting
embracing dark
of a slowly emerging morning.
The fresh, unexpected sunlight
of an October afternoon.
I celebrate this season
of speedy transition
from the lazy sensual days
of the gone too soon summer
to the stimulating, belligerent days
of the exhilarating winter.

Sam Lyons

WINTER'S SONG

Dark branches pointing skyward,
The trees in winter, stand,
Keeping their silent vigil
In a cold and frosty land,
And in those same dark branches,
Birds, seeking shelter, blessed
Through winter's long night watches,
In finding warmth and rest.

The winter's dawn, comes slowly,
And nature holds her breath,
Waiting for the golden orb
To chase night's frozen death,
Then, in a blaze of glory,
The sun peeps o'er the rim,
Making the landscape sparkle,
That had been cold and dim.

And every frost-filled hollow,
And every silent stream
Welcomes the sun's returning,
Fulfilment of a dream,
The dream of winter's ending,
The burgeoning of spring,
The glorious re-awakening,
That makes the whole world, sing.

Nancy Knight

Falling Leaves

The wind buffeted the trees,
sweeping off the autumnal leaves.
Dancing them across the lawn,
as the day began to dawn.
Yellow, gold and amber too,
all the splendid autumn hue.
The last leaves cling until with relief
winds send them to the ground beneath.
Scattered remnants of summer days,
drifting in the sunny haze.
Soon trees will stand with branches bare,
as if the leaves had never been there.
Through wintry weather whatever it may bring,
the trees will sleep and wait for spring.

P Kendrick

HUMANE LIFE CYCLE

Changing seasons are
Like changes in human beings
Conception birth teenage
Adult phase and elderly stage
Of a human existence
Like summer autumn winter spring
From seedling and bulb phase
Colouring colourful
To grown-up stage maturing situation
Every moment every day
Kaleidoscopic life's livings
I simply wonder and wander
Experiencing taking part
In all these guaranteed
Happenings nutritious nutritioning
Colouring colourful to the sight
Imagination wanderings
In unison wholesome whole

Ghazanfer Eqbal

OLD MAN WINTER

Old man winter came along
And stopped me singing summer's song
He changed the scene
And before I knew
The sky was grey instead of blue
The rain came down and lashed the earth
The gutters gurgled
But not in mirth
The wind was howling round the eaves
Then frolicked with the autumn leaves
Naked trees stood stark and cold
Helpless, in old winter's hold
Again the scene was changed and so
The mountain tops were white with snow
While far below
All glittering white
The frost adorned each thing in sight
As I gazed, it wasn't long
Till I was singing winter's song.

Nan Ogg

AUTUMN'S SONG

A joyful song the autumn wind sings
taking the place of winter, summer and spring
blowing leaves from trees, leaving them bare
in the season's clear breezy air.
Carpets of foliage sweeping the ground
with colours bright orange and differing browns.
Autumn renewing her yearly role
embracing the earth, mantled in gold
in her gown that's truly fair.

Jean Parry

SUNDAY PANIC

A rippling stream, a winding track, a warm and sunny day,
white cloth outspread for picnic snack . . . a family at play.
Young boy, engrossed with fishing net; young girl, with kite and line;
high overhead a passing jet flies by with roar and whine.

Mum butters bread and slices cake, Dad busily brews tea,
Grandpa tries hard to stay awake, child sits on Grandma's knee.
Youth lies entranced as Walkman blares, girlfriend threads daisy chain.
Male hiker, passing by, just stares. Companion shows disdain.

Horse canters through steep hillside fields, sheep graze on
lush green grass.
Sun's rays reflect on car windshields as lumbering vehicles pass.
Tired farmer, herding cows, plods on now milking time draws near;
old faithful sheepdog checks none strays nor straggles at the rear.

Leaves rustle in hedgerow and trees, young fledglings soar on high;
Sweet birdsong, carried by the breeze, enchants from clear blue sky.
    Marauding ants to chase away and busy buzzing bee
    but it's a *perfect* summer's day for Sunday picnic tea.

Maureen Atkin

TWO SEASONS IN ONE

If only we could have two seasons
all rolled into one.
Wouldn't it be lovely then
For nearly everyone.
The sun would shine so brightly that
each day from dawn till dusk
our kids could play outside all day
instead of pestering us.
Try to also picture
just what it would be like
if evenings through the summer
were as dark as winter nights.
You could cuddle up to someone
who means a lot to you
and if you're really fortunate
they may respond to you.
But if you feel romantic too
just turn the lights down low
then play a sentimental song
upon your stereo.
The reason why I think these seasons
should become as one
is because we'd have the best of
two worlds for everyone.
The ones who feel too hot by day
could cool off overnight
and those who hate dark evenings
could spend their time outdoors all day
enjoying all the sunshine
as well as all the light.

Merilyn Elizabeth Anne Gulley

SEPTEMBER

September ushers in a time of peace;
the summer sun no longer burns the earth
but, gently, almost lovingly, bestows
its blessing on the upturned heads of flowers
still tearstained from the morning's shower of rain.
Gone now the pastel shades of early spring,
the snowdrops that gave place to daffodils;
sombre the radiant reds and blues of summer,
now faded to the mauve of Michaelmas,
the pink and amber of chrysanthemums.
And though the sun still bathes the world in light
there is a hint of coolness in the air,
a scattering of leaves upon the grass,
and we do well to welcome every day
while autumn lasts, for once its warmth is lost
we must resign ourselves to winter's frost.

Ivy E Russell

FEEDING TIME

A winding stream flowed through the glade;
It was a peaceful scene,
Where larch trees grew and willows too,
With brushwood in between.

Primroses grew beside the stream,
The prey of honey bees;
And a little bird had built a nest
Among the willow trees.

Red squirrel roamed the treetops high;
Alert and bold was he!
His winter store of nuts all gone,
He hunted hungrily.

Then, from above, he spied the nest;
Came quickly to the ground
and scampered up the willow tree
To see what he had found.

Four speckled eggs lay in the nest;
They tasted fresh and good!
Upon the ground he cleaned his paws,
In the silence of the wood.

A keen hawk, watching from on high,
Then hovered overhead;
A flash of wings; a frightened cry;
And red squirrel was dead!

A winding stream flows through the glade;
A sad and lonely scene -
A tuft of fur; an empty nest
Where four small eggs had been.

Eva Morris

My Glorious Day

While walking across the meadows green
Bushes and trees bursting out serene
The birds singing in the trees
Pheasants calling, but not to be seen
Rabbits running from their burrows
Up and down between the furrows
Fir trees in the wood swaying in the breeze
The squirrels running up and down with ease
While underneath the fir trees lay
The cones of yesterday
Some have been nibbled by the mice and voles
And some taken down in their holes
The snowdrops bursting out in bloom
A carpet of white will be seen soon
With the sun shining up above
Flying past, that's a dove
Landing on the trees for the night
That means it's getting late
I'll turn around in case it's waiting for a mate
Once again my walk has ended
Back home sitting in my chair
Thinking of all the things I had seen
No better place I could have been
To my bed I shall sleep
With wonderful thoughts I will keep.

Ivy Blades

First Snow

    A flake spins
as if succulent sweet apple trees
are losing petals to a summer breeze.

    Flakes gather
to skydive in patterns which recall
wild parachuting thistles in freefall.

    Snow eddies
twist; infiltrate path stones in whirling
and scatter wisps like bold ants foraging.

    White strands stream
to flurry these newly blanch'd ant hills
to flowery crescent shapes like crystal frills.

    A dusk wind
howls and hauls the dark evening blizzard
into drifts which threaten daylight hazard.

    A dawn fleece
of sheared sky wool tinsels the black trees
to warm and warn that year's end touch can freeze.

    We see now
gold green weight compelled to bend and bow
in branch obeisance to pale sun with snow.

    I sense too
woodland growth fading with autumn's drip
crisp and congeal in wintry season's grip.

Dennis Marshall

CHANGING SEASONS

'Did you go down Death Valley, Gran?'
Four-year-old eyes obliterate his face.
'Yes Tom, it's really, really deep,
And hot; people down there
Fry eggs on rocks,
And at the very bottom
There's a poison lake
Called 'Badwater'.

I did not say, when we were there,
El Nino's showers had
Strewn the floor with milkweed
And some other, yellow, flowers;
The temperature a
Deadly seventy four.

But sent a postcard back to Tom,
Reflecting, as I licked ice cream,
He too must wait
To lose his dreams.

Sue Knight

A Walk On The Wild Side

As dappled sunlight filters through the glade,
Celandines, their petals closed ranks, rest in the shade.
The ancient oak, with severed bough,
is leaning unsteadily windward, dying now
and yearling saplings, now his end is nigh,
dare to reach their timid branches to the sky.

And high in the regal Scot's pine, scuffling at its crown
a squirrel sends rejected cone remains swirling down,
Then nesting birds call warnings to their mates
as buzzard hovers skyward, checking out the stakes!
Meandering through the woodland is a gently strolling stream
whilst beyond the craggy cliff, the mighty sea now serene.

The woodland path is worn where many feet have strayed,
Nearby bright bluebells in carpets have been laid,
Far into the distance hear the traffic's muted drone -
Paled to insignificance when cocooned in nature's home.

As evening shadows filter through the glade
I find I have retraced the early steps I made,
The day's now done, night creatures come on duty!
As shadows spread the glade takes on a different kind of beauty.

Lynda Burton

THE BEST EXCUSE

Winter though wild - you tame us
To me - you've won your halo
I see you as famous
From the moment you say 'Hello'

I cannot ever wait
For your darkness to fall
So to close the curtain
On your evening call
So cosy for certain

You are our Goliath
Helping with privacy graciously
Shutting out the world -
- Tho' not maliciously

Away from all outside din
Winter you're the best excuse -
- For staying in.

Barbara Sherlow

THE COALS

The cold wind blows through the wintry night,
Just listen to its howling, whistly way.
But the logs upon the fire make the flames
so brilliant, bright.
Watch it burning with such luminous array.

Oh, those coals, those glowing coals.
Just to watch them, warmth enfolds.

See the flicker from the fireside
throwing upwards to the sky.
Spitting, crackling, like the glorious fireflies
prancing with their luminous winglets,
Always dancing, never falter.
Flames like these will surely never die.

Oh, those coals, those glowing coals.
Watch it, see what next it holds.

Then the bright light's flaming colour
casts a shadow all around you,
Making swirling, leaping patterns all afore.
Shimmering, quivering, then they falter,
Fall to just a glowing ember.
Dying ashes that then I am sure.

Oh, those coals, those glowing coals.
Whilst they're burning warmth enfolds.

Jackie Hyde

Seasons' Treasured Moments

Fresh lemon on a summer's day
cool lotion on a burning skin
A blaze of colour transforming views
summer's flora bearing transient hues.

Leaves fall and scatter creating
autumn's carpet
Horse chestnuts rustle as tiny hands
fumble for seasonal prizes
Autumnal breezes transcend paper kites
as people versus wind power
struggle for unknown heights.

Silent blankets of winter's snow
creating uneven landscapes
Seasons music, bells and holy messages
remembering friends past and present
Xmas dinner roast turkey and pheasant.

New life and fresh ideas
future plans for annual events
Spring's exciting introductions
planning, scheming, new adventures
fresh thoughts and renewed attitudes
Preparing oneself for a wholesome New Year
treasured moments and heartfelt cheer.

Mai Clarke

SUMMER IS HERE

At the side of the lake, I sit and ponder,
On this worn out wooden seat,
I thought around the lake I could wander,
But rain, I was unlucky to meet.

Summer is here well and truly this year,
But remember I'm in the North East:
It's different here you see my dear,
Not fit for man or beast.

The water ripples quite quickly on the lake,
Sun lost in the grim grey sky.
A red robin just landed, for goodness sake,
Took one look and away did fly.

The pine trees reach towards the sombre sky,
Rhododendrons, guardians of the lake,
Pink and purple and yellow catch my eye,
As good as icing on a birthday cake.

What is that moving among the tall trees?
Where the picnic tables stand.
Brave families not afraid to freeze,
Massive sandwiches clutched in each hand.

I feel this rain will continue to pour,
So into the car I go.
Along the road - fifty yards, no more,
Sunshine - believe me, it's summer you know.

Dorothy Whitehall

Autumn

Autumn means so many things,
leaves red, gold, and brown,
swallows twittering overhead,
and chestnuts falling down.

Conkers threaded on a string,
blackberry jam for tea,
Crumpets, toasted by the fire
enough, for you and me.

Robin pecking up the crumbs,
ice upon the pool,
lights in windows shining through,
greet children home from school.

Smoke from log fires, drifting high,
Jack Frost upon the pane,
fireworks colouring the sky.
Bright berries down the lane.

Apples picked for winter store,
last rose upon the tree.
All these things, and many more
mean autumn's here, for me.

Joyce Mussett

Autumn Pleasures

I like to see the autumn tints
cascading from the trees,
and sitting in a quiet spot,
with a cool, refreshing breeze.
The holiday crowds now are gone
until next spring skies appear,
and you can go for a quiet stroll
along the promenade or pier.
Porridge oats come to the fore,
hot-pots and stews too,
everything appetising
to warm the hearts of you.
Autumn fares with Christmas ideas
you can get many a good gift there;
then back home to a blazing fire
and your old easy armchair.

Marjorie Cowan

A Garden Thought

Just a little thought when feeling out of sorts
When the burdens weigh quite heavy putting you off course,
Instead of burying your head in the sand
Just look around at God's creations in the land,
Then brace yourself and look towards the months of spring
Enjoy the miracles of nature and everything it brings.
Forget the dark days and all the strife
When the plants and trees come to life,
And the animals come out of hibernation
Waking up to God's Salvation,
Then the birds and bees begin to build their nests and dams
Soon the fields will be full of woolly lambs.
The universe in springtime so fresh and clean
The start of the gardeners' annual scene.
To walk in a garden or over the fields
When spring is in the air, reminds us of God's gifts to yield.

Later the smell of a rose or new mown hay
Helping to drive those traumas away
To see the hand of God at work in everything
Together with the joy and comfort which it can bring
The satisfaction of those garden thoughts
Again reminds us of that special garden where God walks.
So when feeling glum or a little upset
Sit or walk in a garden and you will soon forget
The worries or even the presence of time
Because in a garden you are closer to God which is so divine.

Nancy Owen

Haiku Seasons

Spring Photosynthesis
Breathes life in Nature's flora.
Springtime miracle.

Buds urgently thrust
Towards the sun. Nutrition
Via chlorophyll.

Summer Scented roses climb
Through criss-cross latticework
In peaceful arbour.

Bees and hoverflies
Busy and inquisitive,
Hum in monotone.

'Neath flower-strewn bonnet,
Gentle face in sweet repose,
Absorbing the dream.

Autumn Regal, flame-crowned trees,
In mutual admiration,
Display their beauty.

Strong and thoughtless winds
Scatter their flimsy raiments:
Golden butterflies.

Limbs, denuded, wait,
In silent apprehension,
For winter's onslaught.

Winter   Horizontal glaze
Presses once-green grass to earth
In cold suspension.

Graceful royal waves
From icing sugar branches,
In jewelled ballet.

Marion Evans

WINTER'S HOPE

An alarm clock rings, is it yet spring,
When out of the duvet rise?
Depressing dark days,
When the ice and rain plays
Havoc with our ego's size.

The winter's cold, and damp causes mould,
To be positive needs a surge to produce.
When I herald the dawn,
Waking up with a yawn,
To remain requires no excuse.

It cannot be Monday, was yesterday Sunday,
When I stayed cuddled up forever?
The evening's streetlights,
The days are not that bright,
Raw rewards for too much endeavour!

The nights get less, the sun's longer in the west
Suddenly it is spring at last.
Daffodils are seen,
Snowdrops, planted runner beans,
Last season's clothes return - with a fast.

The warmth of the sun, budding trees and birdsong,
Walks, small lambs, scented air.
Looking forward to sunrise,
Sunsets with reddish skies,
New life, new hope from despair.

Blazing hot days, countryside, fields and hay,
Roses, wedding poses in June.
Life's a wonderful thing,
Like the bird on the wing,
Freedom, longed for summer honeymoon.

Barrie W Neate

Beautiful Autumn

I wonder why the dear Lord made autumn
The most beautiful season of them all?
The time when plump fruits and red berries come
To load trees before their russet leaves fall.
Crisp autumn is a time of fulfilment,
Harvest shows the dear Lord has blessed the seed,
Soft spring rain and summer sunshine, He sent
To provide fruits of the earth that we need.
As crisply bronzed leaves swirl onto the soil,
Little creatures harvest their winter store,
And men look for rest after summer toil,
On long sunny days, having closed the door.
But in such beauty in fall and decay,
God promises rebirth in spring's new days.

Pat Heppel

NATURE'S WONDERS

On this earth, you surely know;
'God's Creation - in abundance shows'

Wild seeds scattered in the fields;
'Wondrous crops our farmers do yield'

Poppies grow - in summertime;
'All nature's wonders are divine'

Golden leaves - in autumn time;
'Passing seasons all in rhyme'

White crystals come in wintertime;
'Nature's beauty all divine'

All God's beauty, 'here to see'
'Nature provideth for you and me' . . .

Valerie Baker (Valerian Poems)

THE FOUR SEASONS

Spring Sweet Spring,
when April showers
bring
forth May flowers,
and birds sing.

Summer Children play,
the weather's fine
everyday;
in the sunshine,
farmers make hay.

Autumn Gales blow,
and the leaves
go
up my sleeves -
just like so.

Winter It snows;
a cold breeze
blows
through the trees,
and I'm froze.

Roger Williams

SNOW IN WINTER

One morning in winter
I sit in the kitchen
here at home alone
comfortable and settled
with the world outside
covered with a thick drift of snow
It is brisk and cold
in the kitchen
as I look at the whiteness outside
but that does not worry me
Cold as it is
as for snow I am glad to be alive

Lynne Heather West

WINGS AND THINGS

Ah! Bright winds and things of summer
bringing joy to many children.
Filtered sunrays bringing magic
to each corner of the garden.

Blackbirds race across the grassland
feasting on the fallen apples.
Small lambs gambol on the hillside,
happy springing, bouncing creatures.

Cycling homeward in the evening,
summer breezes gently cooling.
Fill the heart with such elation
then home to dream, of golden days.

Pam Dawkins

AUTUMN DAWN

My past, my present, my future,
my yesterday and my tomorrow.
Regrets that mingle with the mist.
The words that I had to borrow.
Even if anybody forgave me
I have never forgiven myself.
Thoughts blow with the leaves
as I cling to them like an elf.
Feeling small makes that easy
staring across the autumn dawn.
I've been blowing in the wind
since the day that I was born.

David J Burke

Seasons' Reasons

The wind will blow
To shake the leaves,
Whistling sounds
Insects on knees
Fear of being blown away -
Lost upon the wind till May.

G Gray

THEY TELL ME SPRING IS BEAUTIFUL

They tell me Spring is beautiful, and wondrous to behold,
As from dull winter's brown and grey, a myriad hues unfold.
That buds are bursting on the trees, to form a canopy
Of delicate leaf-tracery - a beauteous panoply.

They tell me birds are soaring high, with jewelled wings unfurled;
That rays of morning sun reveal a richly coloured world.
They say the sky is heav'nly blue; that grass is tender green;
That water ripples in clear streams where ice had solid been.

They tell me that in verdant fields the frisking lambs are seen -
Their wriggling, corkscrew tails abob, beside the ewes serene.
That yellow celandines upturn their faces to the air,
While pure white snowdrops bow their heads, as if in quiet prayer.

They tell me Spring is beautiful, and really they are kind,
Because they know I cannot see - my sightless eyes are blind.
But - I can *hear* the sounds of Spring, and *smell* the sweet
                                                    Spring scents,
And *stroke* the creatures; *touch* the flowers, and *feel* the elements.

Yet what they tell me, has upon my inner eye designed
A masterpiece, created on the canvas of my mind.
They tell me Spring is beautiful, and this is manifest
Within my soul - *I see it all* - with inner vision blest.

Eileen N Blackmore

Autumn

There is russet brown, and there's gold and green,
And ruby red and orange can be seen,
A splash of bright colours are all around,
The trees with such wondrous beauty are crowned.

Underfoot a carpet that's crisp and brown,
The chestnuts and beechnuts are falling down,
And acorns are scattered around the trees,
And the leaves are blown around in the breeze.

The squirrels are gathering in their store,
And the nuts are yet falling more and more,
A chill is now lingering on the air,
The bitter winter cold is almost here.

Into burrows and dens animals creep,
Through the cold winter months many will sleep,
The days become short, and the nights grow long,
Plants will sleep in the earth where they belong.

Leaves and flowers are dying one by one,
For the season's cycle is never done,
Very soon the trees will be stark and bare,
And not a touch of brightness anywhere.

For they all await resurrection morn,
When all of creation will be reborn,
As we also await that coming day,
When the kingdom of our Lord will hold sway.

Ruth Dewhirst

CHANGING SEASON

Wake up to start a fresh new day,
To see sunshine gleaming through your window.
Only you can feel the season,
Only you can experience joy.

Step out into the sunlit world,
As today could bring new meaning.
The light reflects through blooming trees,
Inspiration enlightens your path.

The endless glow of summer,
Will enhance your frozen spirits.
The feel of warm tenderness,
Is soon to die so cold.

Spirits will soon dampen,
Around dew and clouds of mist.
Time can be so deceiving,
Although changing seasons will soon combine.

E Snell

THE FALL

In the marshmallow twilight
The evening chill takes hold
And the air smells of a smokiness
And stories are often told
Of an Indian summer magic
When pumpkins seem to smile
With eyes that are lit by candles
And somehow for a while
The world has the strangest nature
Falling leaves of gold and red
And clear starlit nights
To light our way to bed

Autumn, season of contrast
You surprise me every day
Sometimes as mellow as summer
Other times winter grey

But most of all I remember
Our wedding day's morning mist
Changing magically to sunshine
The moment that we kissed.

B King

AUTUMN

Golden hues drift aimlessly down from a sea-blue sky,
only to be carried along on a whirly burly tide of
autumn colour. Which beaches in every corner
and around every tree, while gentle autumn sirens,
call softly foretelling of things to come.

Down through the resplendent trees, the aromatic
scent of a thousand bonfires, fills the cool air
with its incense like beauty. A beauty only
to be surpassed, by the ambrosial fragrance
of a quiet summer meadow.

As the cool sulphureous sun sets gently behind
the far distant hills, the thin vales of mist
begin to rise. Weaving its way from meadow to mead
without a single sound. Leaving all but the faintest
hint of dew, which glistens on every tree and flower.

When as the last lights of day fade into night
and the autumnal sirens have fallen silent. The harvest
moon with its celestial glow, rises to silhouette
Mother Nature's earthy gown, with a silky radiance.
So beautiful that words cannot describe.

Ever so soon autumn's melancholy splendour, is once
more illuminated by the gentle morning sun.
The mist now fades into a memory, leaving all but
the dew, that glistens like a million tiny diamonds.
To see this is to see your life personified to its full glory.

Andrew Whitfield

Autumn Leaves

Leaves falling in the autumn breeze
dropping from the deciduous trees.
Like gold dust falling from the sky,
this leaf formation to the eye.

Leaves of red, yellow, brown and gold,
glisten in the sunlight's hold.
While our human vision unfolds,
changing shades of autumn gold.

Leaves blowing down from branch to ground,
softly landing with no sound.
Then gently rising in the autumn breeze,
showering glistening colours of autumn leaves.

John Hickman

INFORMATION

We hope you have enjoyed reading this book - and that you will continue to enjoy it in the coming years.

If you like reading and writing poetry drop us a line, or give us a call, and we'll send you a free information pack.

Write to :-
**Triumph House Information
1-2 Wainman Road
Woodston
Peterborough
PE2 7BU
(01733) 230749**